Henry Hawkinson

A message on the fundamental principles of protection, free trade and the Constitution of the United States

Henry Hawkinson

A message on the fundamental principles of protection, free trade and the Constitution of the United States

ISBN/EAN: 9783337277727

Printed in Europe, USA, Canada, Australia, Japan

Cover: Foto ©Suzi / pixelio.de

More available books at **www.hansebooks.com**

A

MESSAGE

ON THE

Fundamental Principles

OF

PROTECTION,

FREE TRADE

AND THE

CONSTITUTION OF THE UNITED STATES.

SEATTLE, WASH.

ACME PUBLISHING COMPANY.

1895.

INTRODUCTION

BY THE AUTHOR.

AS IT seems to be a " great necessity," and also in style, to write messages, I take the liberty of presenting my views to the public on the Fundamental Principles of Protection, Free Trade, and the Constitution of the United States, under the title, " A MESSAGE." My message will be written for *your* special benefit, and I beg of you to read carefully every word it contains before you condemn or accept the principles it upholds.

It is not only a privilege, but our *duty as true and loyal citizens* of the United States, to throw aside all party prejudices ; to educate ourselves to investigate and learn the fundamental principles of Protection, of Free Trade, and the Constitution of the United States. Our form of government is supposed to be a government of the people, by the people, for the people ; therefore, as true and loyal citizens it is our *sworn* duty to see that the fundamental principles of our constitution are not tampered with ; also to retrace and amend every mistake that violates those principles. The oath

of allegiance to our constitution is just as
sacred with a private individual as with the
President or any representative of the people.
Every citizen of the United States has taken
upon himself the, duty to uphold and abide by
the fundamental principles of our constitution.
It is left for the reader to decide what the teachings of those principles mean.

The subjects mentioned are not only the
leading subjects for our investigation, but
Protection and Free Trade are two different
principles of government for our consideration
and choice ; therefore, one of the two must be
good and the other bad. That which is right
can not be wrong ; that which is wrong can not
be right! That which is just can not be unjust, and anything that is unjust cannot be
just. Therefore either Protection or Free Trade
is wrong, and one of the two is right. Half
right and half wrong can not be right ; but it
can be, and always is, wrong ; it is worse than
all wrong : for then we could not be deceived.
That which is in harmony with Nature is just
and natural ; that which is not in harmony
with Nature is fictitious, unjust and unnatural.
If you throw away Nature's best teachings,
what have you but fiction ? Either Protection
or Free Trade is fictitious, and one of the two
just and natural, for they are in direct opposi-
tion to each other ; they can not be mixed,
and when we try to have both at the same time

it is a thousand times worse than the worst of the two alone.

Reader, if you can, please lay aside all partiality long enough to read this message thoroughly and with care ; but if you can not, it will be better for you to lay it aside at once, and not read another word.

If you know the fundamental principles of Protection, Free Trade and the Constitution of the United States thoroughly, my message will be unnecessary. But do you?

My principal object, while presenting my views to the public, will be to present them in plain, every-day language, so that no person who can read can misunderstand them. I do not intend to show partiality to any political party ; I have no reasons for doing so. I have no pet, and I can assure you that I will not handle their principles without the lash. If you are one of the guilty, take your medicine like a man—it will do you good.

Yours for Justice, Prosperity, Domestic Tranquility and General Welfare,

"A SUCKER."

A MESSAGE.

IN GETTING at the foundation or original cause of any thing that we do not fully comprehend, it is always necessary to use Nature, and Nature's best teachings, for beyond Nature is beyond our comprehension. We are, therefore, subjects of Nature's laws, or Nature's best teachings, even if there is an unknown or supreme power, or a ruler of Nature. To become truly intelligent human beings we must make up our minds that we are free agents mentally, and subject to no human dictatorship. No human being has a right to demand that we believe the way he or she does ; and we have no right, as free mental agents and intelligent human beings, to believe the way some other person does, until we have investigated that other person's belief or statement thoroughly and find it true and just.

Reader, did you ever hear of a liar, or dream of one ; did you ever know one person that never —never told a lie ? have you never—never told a lie yourself? The best and noblest men that ever lived have been mistaken in some things, if they never told a lie. No human being is infallible. But you may ask how it is possible for you to investigate the statements made by every one. I will answer by asking other questions.

Did you ever read the contents of the Constitution
of the United States thoroughly and with care?
Did you ever read and compare each amendment to the Constitution to see if it was in
perfect harmony with the fundamental principles? What is the greatest necessity to promote general welfare, happiness and prosperity?
I answer, Good, honest, impartial government,
the foundation, the fundamental principles of
our Constitution.

Did you ever study the fundamental principles
of Protection and Free Trade, to see if they harmonize with the fundamental principles of our
Constitution? If not, why not? How much of
your valuable time would it take to do so? If you
have never done so, I can say honestly and with
all candor, that your political education is fictitious, and that which is fictitious is dangerous, to
yourself and all humanity. The only true and
reliable education is a *personal* knowledge of facts;
a knowledge and education in harmony with
Nature. Nature is the only reliable store-house
of knowledge. Use Nature's greatest law—cause
and effect—in all your investigations.

What was the cause, and what was or will be
the effect?

Always remember, that only a few hundred
years ago our ancestors were heathen savages
and barbarians. And farther back, history
tells us, that they were civilized, educated and
intelligent human beings. Why did they de-

generate and again fall back into ignorance and savagery? Because they had been governed with fictitious laws ; because they had been deprived of every opportunity to advance. Fictitious laws and religions were used by their dictators to shackle their mental liberty. They were not allowed to educate themselves, but were forced to listen to, and believe what their dictators told them. Our present development in intellect is the result of untramelled thought and investigation in harmony with the requirements of Nature, and Nature's laws. Nature's law of cause and effect has been our teacher ; and yet we have fictitious laws and teachings to fight against at all times. These facts alone are enough to prove that Nature's laws are the strongest, if unmuzzled, and that only Nature's laws should be our guide to better the condition of humanity and our government. Nature's laws and teachings, in harmony with Nature, are the only teachings that make men and women truly noble, just and honest! Fictitious teachings make them dishonest, unjust and selfish—and these are the greatest faults with humanity to-day; not in the United States alone, but the world over.

Reader, I do not ask you to believe any of my statements until you have investigated them thoroughly ; and you have no right to deny them until you have investigated and do not find them true and just. I may be mistaken, but I invite criticism, and will answer any criticism, that does not cause me unnecessary expense.

The laws of Nature govern our whole being, our very existence. The laws of Nature govern the whole universe. Nothing can exist that is not in harmony with Nature. From the tiniest plant in vegetation to the mightiest monarchs or rulers of humanity, some day they must all bow in submission to the laws of Nature. When Nature commands they must all obey. When Nature has done its duty, and is done, the mighty monarch must die; his days and hours are sometimes lengthened; but how? Not by fictitious means; not contrary to Nature or Nature's laws.

Drugs, Nature's productions, are used to stimulate, strengthen and prolong life. Nature's stronger elements must be used in harmony with the weaker to stimulate and strengthen the weaker. Drugs are Nature's productions exclusively. In the first place, they are taken from vegetation, minerals, life and animal matter of nearly every description, which are Nature's productions; but you might ask, How are they taken from minerals, vegetation, etc.? By Nature's grandest production on earth—man and woman. But how did man and woman get their intelligence? From Nature—Nature is the only reliable storehouse of knowledge. Through necessity, cause and effect, man and woman have acquired their knowledge and intelligence to use Nature's productions in harmony with the requirements of Nature. You might say that an Almighty God created man and woman—which I do not deny—but as it is utterly impossible for man and woman to exist aside from Nature, that Almighty God certainly made them a part of Nature, to live in harmony with Nature, for without Nature's aid they can not exist. That God certainly must be a God of Nature! If you believe that an Almighty God created everything—the whole universe, everything that we perceive, everything that we call Nature—that God certainly takes a great interest in Nature and must certainly be a God of Nature ; the ideals of his creation, man and woman, cannot exist aside from Nature. Then how can any person contradict my statement that if there be a God, that God is a God of Nature. Science, or Nature's education, has taught us that a person's life can be prolonged and that he will be happier and more contented if the habits of the person's life have been governed by the laws of Nature.

Reader, I sincerely believe that if the life of a person, or any part of Nature, can be governed by and in harmony with the requirements of Nature, that a nation can also be governed in harmony with the requirements of Nature.

Nature is the only original source of education ; anything contrary to Nature's teachings is fictitious. All laws that do not harmonize with Nature's laws are fictitious, Fictitious teachings make hypocrites and dishonest people. Fictitious laws make a dishonest form of government.

If a person is stubborn or through ignorance, "the result of fictitious teachings," contradicts the requirements of his nature, there is danger. Nature has taught us that certain vegetation is dangerous if used for food. Therefore we should not use such vegetation for food, as they would not only shorten our lives but would make us miserable for life; or if very poisonous would extinguish our lives at once. A person can educate himself, fictitiously, to use poisonous drugs, and we see no immediate danger, but the danger is there. He has used fictitious means to stimulate life and his life has been shortened thereby.

So it is with a nation : Fictitious laws, contrary to the requirements of man's nature ; unnatural laws for the purpose of controlling a nation in an unnatural way, are like the poisonous drug, they will either shorten the life of the nation or they will shorten the life of that fictitious, poisonous form of government.

Nature must harmonize. Nature's laws are like a fine piece of machinery which seems quite complicated to the common minds who have not dared to allow Nature and Nature's laws to have complete control of their intellect and education ; who have allowed fictitious and superstitious doctrines and teachings to poison their minds, which are exclusively the result of the teachings of tyrannical and wicked rulers and dictators. Beware of any and all teachings that do not harmonize with Nature or Nature's education and laws ; they are, and have always been, the curse of humanity. Every part of this great natural machine must work in harmony with Nature's laws or there is danger. Like the great locomotive, if there is no escape for the surplus steam the boiler will explode and the combination of the machine is ruined. History tells us of very powerful nations that are no longer in existence. The downfall of the Roman Empire, the downfall of every great nation that has existed since the dawn of history, can be directly traced to the cause of an unnatural and fictitious form of government.

You may ask, Why do I mingle nature with politics ? My friend, the fundamental principles of the Constitution of the United States are the very pearls of Nature's teachings, and if these fundamental principle of our Constitution had been carried out to the letter, I am willing to *stake my life* that there would be no discontented or harsh feeling against our government to-day from true and loyal citizens of the United States. The fundamental principles of our Constitution give no special privileges to any religious doctrine, they all have a privilege to worship in their own way ; the fundamental principles of our Constitution give no special privileges to any man or woman, but it grieves me to be obliged to say that we have several amendments to the Constitution that are fictitious, that conflict with and are a direct violation of the fundamental principles of our Constitution. They are unconstitutional amendments, and if tried even in a justice court would be found unconstitutional. I would like to see the day when no amendment to the Constitution could be presented to Congress before it had gone through a test, in some of the principal courts of the United States, to prove them constitutional or unconstitutional.

The Constitution of the United States is like a seed taken from some good fruit-bearing tree. It was planted with the expectation that the seed would produce another fruit tree, and the tree should bear fruit abundantly. The tree has grown from one year to another until it has become a large and beautiful tree to look upon. But from some unnatural cause the tree only bears fruit on one limb. As the tree will only bear fruit on one limb, it is not a good fruit tree, although it may be beautiful to look upon. Fruit should grow on all of the limbs on every branch, otherwise the tree it not doing justice and credit to the seed that was planted, and there has been some unnatural cause for the result obtained. The seed was good but the result not good. Now let me ask, Which is the best way to apply a remedy for the evil?

Some, no doubt, would say, pull the tree up by the roots and plant another seed, and be sure that you plant a good one. But, my friend, you

A MESSAGE. 15

must consider that you would be wasting time, and the result might be even more disastrous than the first experiment. Some unnatural cause may again prevent that seed from becoming a creditable fruit-bearing tree, and in the mean time you might be starving for fruit. Science, or Nature's education, has taught us that other fruit-bearing limbs can be engrafted in a tree, and that the seed of the tree (the seed of experience) is even better than it ever was, and that simply some unnatural cause in the development of the tree has been the cause of our disappointment. We all know that to make the tree a good and perfect fruit-bearing tree, we must first cut the tree off below the limbs and then proceed to engraft good fruit-bearing limbs, limbs that we know will bear fruit, and we will not be obliged to wait long for good results, for fruit.

The fundamental principles of our Constitution are like seeds taken from good fruit. The fundamental principles of the Constitution of the United States are perfect. They are the pearls of Nature's education ; they are natural and just principles. But what has been the result of that good seed, planted in good soil ; yes, I repeat, in good soil? No better country exists on the face of the earth than the United States. The seed grew ; it has become a gigantic and surely a beautiful tree to look upon, but from some unnatural cause the fruit is all growing on one limb —the limb of mammon. What is the remedy ?

There is only one just and perfect remedy that
can give the very best results to the nature of the
seed that has been planted. It is not just or
necessary that any unnatural cause shall prevent
any limb from bearing fruit abundantly; therefore the unnatural cause must be removed and
Nature's best remedy applied.

The Protective Tariff is fictitious; it is unnatural and unjust. Protection is the foundation
of every evil that exists, and the only just and
natural remedy is absolute Free Trade. Free
Trade for a government is Nature's only fundamental law, and anything contrary is fictitious,
which I hope to prove in such a way as to leave
no room for doubt. The tree must be cut off
below the limbs; and with absolute Free Trade
the limb of every industry in the United States
will be engrafted into the fundamental principles
of our Constitution. If we have laws and amendments to our Constitution in harmony with
Nature's best teaching, the fundamental principles of our Constitution, every limb of industry
in the United States, that is not fictitious, will
prosper and bear fruit abundantly. All fictitious
industries should perish from the face of the
earth, and the sooner the better for humanity.
The Protective Tariff is a fictitious and unjust
form of taxation, and a direct violation of the
fundamental principles of the Constitution of the
United States, and has been the protector for all

of the principal evils that exist in the United States, and the world, to-day.

Every law or form of government that seems complicated to the common minds, and in reality is complicated, have been made so with some designing purpose in view, and is, therefore, fictitious and unnatural. Nature's laws are the simplest laws in existence. If you wish to be just in your dealings with your fellow-man, and wish to do what is right, is it not an easy matter to find out what is right ? Are not the laws of justice and right the simplest laws in existence ? They are Nature's best teachings, Nature's laws, and can not be complicated. But if you wish to be dishonest—to do some fellow-man an injustice —you must overcome your nature, fictitiously; to be able to look him in the eye to tell a lie to deceive him. It takes practice to become a good liar ; it takes practice to become a good confidence man. Most men can never overcome their nature, and be able to tell a lie with an honest-appearing countenance. It is the nature of every human being to be honest, and only a fictitious education makes them dishonest. I BLAME NO MAN for being dishonest, who has been educated fictitiously, and who has been educated in a country that is governed with fictitious laws.

If a person is working for you, and you wish to make a large and unreasonable profit off his labors, you must contradict Nature ; you must lie to mislead him ; you must scheme and manage

in different ways to keep him in ignorance of
your actual income or profits. But if you wish
to be honest; if you wish to give that person a
just recompense for the result of his labors, you
will use Nature's greatest law : justice. You will
have no scheming or underhanded problems to
figure out to accomplish your object. Show me
a law that is so complicated that it is almost impossible to comprehend, and I will show you a
fictitious law, with some designing purpose in
view. It can not be just and complicated, but
has become a law for the purpose of robbing, or
taking advantage of persons who least expect it.

Show me a simple form of law and I will show
you a just and natural law. Honesty is simplicity. Where honesty, simplicity, justice and intelligence are combined, is where you will find
the highest order of civilization. Are we half
civilized ? Just stop a moment, and think of it.
Is there not room for improvement ?

A government that has just and natural fundamental laws, that have not been tampered with,
need never fear revolutions or discontent among
the people towards that government. The history of any extinct government will prove to you
without a doubt that fictitious and unjust laws
and legislation was the cause of the disasters that
came over them.

When people say that it is impossible to have
a perfect, just and pure government, they say so
through ignorance. They have received a ficti-

tious education and are not to blame for their ignorance. I would advise such persons to give Nature's best teachings full control of their intellect ; to use Nature's law of cause and effect in their investigations, and their education will be based on facts. A pure, just and perfect form of government can exist. The fundamental principles of our Constitution are just, and that which is just is perfect, and in harmony with Nature's best teachings. But unjust, fictitious and unconstitutional laws have been passed by our legislators ever since the foundation of the Constitution, and they are the cause of the present depressed condition in the United States. With unjust and underhanded forms of taxation, caused by unjust and dishonest legislation, the people are at all times forced to be on the defensive or starve. Is not that enough to cause discontent among the people ? One scheme after another is hatched in Congress for the purpose of aiding capital to rob the people. The whole present system is a fictitious and unjust one, for the purpose of shifting the burden of taxation from the capitalist onto the shoulders of the producers and consumers, which I expect to prove to the reader in such a way as to leave no room for contradiction.

What I would like to impress upon the minds of the people more particularly is the following : That the citizens of the United States have permitted congress to pass unjust and fictitious laws without making a noticeable murmur. Instead

of rising up in combined strength at the polls to
kick the rascals out, we have been so partisan as
to allow party loyalty and prejudice to control our
ballot ; and instead of kicking them out we have
elected them for another term, with even a larger
majority.

I have personally heard many a good Republican say that he would rather vote for a Republican whom he knew was a rascal, than to vote
for a Democrat, no matter how honest the Democrat may be.   And I have heard Democrats make
the same remarks about Republicans ; and the
result has been that the leaders in both the old
parties are nearly all rascals, robbers, gamblers
and thieves.   My friends, this may sound like a
very reckless assertion, but I can prove to you in
a very few words that I am telling the truth.   It
takes a rascal to be a good robber.   The leaders
of your party have robbed you of your confidence
in them, for they have given you nothing in
return.   They have robbed you of your birth-
right in the United States, and they are gambling
every day with the products of your labor and
the necessities of life.   When an intelligent people, like the people of the United States, become
so careless and dormant as to allow other people
to think for them, and dictate their ballot for
them, there is danger ; especially when the Constitution of the United States has given them the
special privilege of untrammelled thought and free
speech, and a right to vote.   It is a disgrace to

the nation that they have not taken more interest in the general welfare of humanity. In the end they, or their posterity, will suffer the consequences.

THE PROTECTIVE TARIFF

AND THE

CONSTITUTION OF THE UNITED STATES.

WE will now see what the object was in framing the Constitution of the United States, and see if the object has been carried out. The following contains the object or fundamental principles of our Constitution :

We, the people of the United States, in order to form a more perfect union, establish justice, insure domestic tranquility, provide for the common defense, promote general welfare and secure the blessings of liberty, to ourselves and our posterity, do ordain and establish this Constitution for the United States of America.

I will ask of you, as a special favor to yourself, not to forget the word "justice," the greatest word in the English language : and there could

be no better place for that word than in the Constitution of the United States. Please take into
consideration the meaning of "general welfare.'

Before we proceed to investigate the Protective
Tariff system, I wish to state to the reader that I
am not a Democrat, and not a Republican ; but
an absolute Free Trader, and will prove to you
that the Protective Tariff is unconstitutional.

I am a poor man, but I will willingly give one
hundred dollars to any man in the United States
who can prove that the United States ever had
absolute Free Trade; and when it is not absolute, it
is not Free Trade.

The law of supply and demand should be the
only law to regulate or govern the price of any
article, no matter whether it be a necessity of life
or a luxury. The common laborer is entitled to
luxuries that he can afford to have, just as much
as the President of the United States, and he
should have a comparitive opportunity, or as
nearly so as it could be possible.

I condemn every import duty as an unjust
form of taxation ; in conflict with the "general
welfare" of the people, and the object of the Constitution to promote "general welfare." Import
duties give that which is taxed a fictitious value,
and give the products of American producers an
inferior value. Both the producer and consumer
is robbed, besides every man who is not directly
benefitted by Protection, or import duties. The
producer is obliged to sell the products of his

labor for less than their real value whether they
are sold at home or abroad. We all know that
the Liverpool markets rule the markets of the
world. Therefore, remember that the price of
your product is made according to the price at
Liverpool, no matter where you sell that product
so long as the smallest percentage of that same
product enters foreign markets. The American
farmer is robbed of his profit on every bushel of
wheat, corn or any other cereal or product that
ever enters foreign markets.

If an American or English trader or merchant
enters into the business of dealing in American
wheat (or any other cereal), he certainly enters
into the business for a profit. It don't matter
where he intends to ship the wheat, the Liverpool market rules the market price of our wheat,
less the expense of shipping. If the vessel to be
used is owned by an American, it will of course
start with the cargo of wheat from one of our
ports. Any man with common sense knows that
it is impossible for a freight vessel to cross the
ocean, empty. The vessel must have ballast of
some kind, or it would be utterly impossible for
the vessel to cross. On account of our Protective
Tariff, all of the expense attached to the trip to
Europe, and back again, must be charged exclusively, or almost exclusively, to the cargo of
wheat.

First of all the dealer gets the market price of
American wheat at Liverpool. To be sure that

he can return, for another cargo of wheat, he
must take into consideration the return trip.
The first item to be charged up against a cargo of
wheat, is freight to Liverpool. If the trader de-
cides to take ballast for the return trip, another
freight is charged against the wheat, besides the
expense attached to loading and unloading the
ballast. And I ask, Who pays the freight? The
original producer, the farmers and every man
who labors for a living. All the expense attached to shipping the wheat must be charged
up before the trader buys the wheat. Does your
local buyer make you a price on your wheat before he first consults the market, and adds freight
to the nearest market? But if the trader takes
merchandise for ballast, for the return trip, then
an import duty to Uncle Sam must be added besides the freight. This must all be charged
against the cargo of wheat before they can make
us a price on our wheat or any other cereal or
product of any kind.

It is not enough that the American producers
and laborers pay this extra price on the cereals
that are sold in European countries, but they pay
it on every bushel and on every pound that is
sold and consumed at home, even if fed to the
hogs. Only from five to ten per cent. of our products are sold abroad, but the price of the other
ninety per cent., or whatever it might be, is
always controlled according to the Liverpool
markets, less the expense of shipping both ways,
and import duties, or ballast charges.

So long as there is an import duty in exist-ence, the expense of shipping our products to foreign markets must always first be charged to our products. Now, candidly, do the English manufacturers pay the expense of getting that wheat? Does the Englishman pay the import duty on the merchandise brought to this country? Do you, an intelligent human being, think that the English manufacturers are so ignorant that they would bring a cargo of merchandise and sell to us below cost, just for the sake of buying our wheat and other products? Do you think they would bring a cargo of merchandise and pay an import duty to Uncle Sam, at a loss to them-selves? No, my friend; the Englishman is not so ignorant as that. He would always charge that duty to your products which he buys for the return trip.

I will give one hundred dollars to any man in the United States who can prove that England, Germany, France, or any other country on the face of the earth, ever pays a duty to Uncle Sam that is not already charged to the American pro-ducers and consumers, in an indirect way.

They do not pay Uncle Sam, they only loan him the money at a' most damnable high rate of interest, until they buy our products for the return trip. The statement made by Republican and Protective Tariff Democrats, that they do pay the duty, and that it does not interfere with the price of our products, is the most damnable lie

that human being ever breathed. It is a disgrace
to American intelligence to believe such statements. It is an insult to American intelligence
tnat any person should stand up in public and
make such a statement.

, My friend, it is not enough that the American
producers pay the tariff on the merchandise
brought from foreign countries ; but the producer,
consumer and laboring men pay a duty on the
products of our own manufactures. But this duty
does not go to the support of our government.
The Protective Tariff is supposed to be just high
enough to keep out foreign competition; therefore
our manufacturers take advantage of this Protective Tariff and raise the price of their product,
from its actual value to the same level as the
import duty added to foreign merchandise, and
the higher the Protective Tariff is, the better it is
for manufacturers. They can raise the price of
their products whenever the Tariff is raised, and
the original producers and the consumers pay
every cent of it, just for the sake of creating a new
millionaire for each month in the year ; and for
the sake of becoming poorer every year ; and for
getting a chance to pay these same millionaires
a high rate of interest for the use of their money
—the money that would be yours if we had
absolute Free Trade. You also pay this extra
price for the sake of having a heavy mortgage on
your home.

There are very few farmers in the United

States to-day, who own their farms free of incumbrance, that did not have a clear title before our late war, or over thirty years ago. Possibly you, dear reader, have lived for twenty-five or thirty years with a plaster on your farm or home. You have been saving, you have economized, for the sake of paying off this mortgage, but instead of paying it off, you have been obliged to renew the mortgage from time to time. You feel discouraged ; you lose confidence in yourself ; but still you go to the polls and continue to vote for the *curse* that hangs over you, that hangs over your posterity. You are voting for your own damnation, and the damnation of your children. A terrible disaster is now hanging over our heads, can we avoid it ? I say that we can if we will all join hands, in 1896, to down the greatest curse to humanity that can exist !

Reader, do you know that for one hundred years the fundamental principles of our Constitution have been buried deep in oblivion? Give me the fundamental principles of our Constitution ; give me the privilege of repealing every amendment that does not harmonize with those principles ; give me absolute Free Trade, which is in harmony with the fundamental principles of our Constitution ; give me a law to provide for a test of every amendment offered, to the Constitution, before it may be presented to Congress, and I know positively that the United States of America will be the most prosperous country or

nation that has existed since the dawn of history.
If present conditions continue much longer we
will be the slaves of a monarchy and despotism.
But more of this later. We will give Protection,
a more thorough analysis.

Import duties are unjust ; they conflict with
the general welfare of the p·ople ; they conflict
with every law of justice that exists ; they conflict with the law of supply and demand. All
import duties stagnate trade ; they stagnate our
commercial intercourse with tne balance of the.
world, but our import duties, or the Protective
Tariff, is what has made our millionaires—at our
expense.

The Protective Tariff is not a desirable form
of taxation for the support of any government.
It is the most, expensive and most complicated
form of taxation in existence, and therefore certainly is an unjust form of taxation. It does not
keep the government treasury filled. The government has been obliged to issue bonds, from
one time to another, for the last thirty years, to
keep the necessary amount of money in the treasury. Why should it be thus, when the people of
the United States are virtually paying a Protective Tariff that amounts to billions of dollars per
annum? The Protective Tariff can only be for
the one purpose : that of aiding capital ; to
strengthen combines, trusts and monopolies. As
laboring men and original producers of wealth,
we pay every dollar that goes for the support of

,our government,. We expect to do so! How can
a non-creator of wealth do so? ·He can not!
Therefore we have a right to see that our government affairs are judiciously managed. We have
a right to condemn a vicious system of taxation
that is cursing us every day of our lives, even if
we did at one time think it was right. We live
to learn, and the man that does not learn something every day of his life is an idiot or a fool.
The man who thinks his father knows everything
that is worth knowing is a fool. The father who
don't want his children to know any more than
he does is a fool. If it had not been for religious
liberty, untrammeled thought and free speech,
what would be our condition to-day as human
beings?

My friend, the Protective Tariff is the greatest
robbery in existence! It robs every farmer and
producer in the United States ; it robs every merchant and business man ; and every professional
man or woman, no matter what their profession
may be. When the original producer of wealth
is robbed, we are all robbed. If the original producers are making money, there is always more
money to enter the local channels of business.
The farmer don't want money just for itself any
more than you do ; but he wants wealth—that
which money is merely a representative of, or
merely an agent, to facilitate distribution of
wealth. If you have everything else that you
need, what do you want money for? What good

would a large amount of money do you locked up in your closet, or trunk, or in a bank? You simply want money to buy something that will add to your wealth and comfort. Money in itself is not wealth; it is merely a temporary representative. We have over three hundred millionaires in the United States, who are worth billions upon billions of dollars, but their wealth is not represented with money. There is very little money in the hands of these capitalists, therefore, even they, the very best financiers, do not consider money wealth. It is merely what money represents that they want: land, property, merchandise, or a mortgage on your home; you may have the money if you give them an interest in your home.

When the farmers, or original producers, are not making any money, or accumulating wealth, how can others expect to? When the very foundation of wealth, the creators of wealth, have no wealth, how can you expect that you can accumulate it to-day and expect that it shall have the same value to-morrow? The farmers and original creators of wealth are the gilt edge securities of your wealth. Why has your property, your wealth, depreciated in value, my friend? Simply because the gilt edge security for it has depreciated in value. The "great robber"—Protection —has depreciated the value of your security by robbing the original producers of their profits while you have been asleep. And I will stake my life that your property cannot increase in value until the security behind it is guaranteed. Fictitious and temporary securities have been placed before you for the last twenty years or more. They have been simply promissory notes that are worthless, and the only securities you have to-day are the farmers and original producers. Provide means to increase their wealth and you increase your own. If the creators of wealth are not creating it, how can you expect wealth.

Protective Tariff has simply been giving large combines and capitalists an opportunity to gamble with you to see who should have the wealth that has already been created, and they are very successful because Protection gives them a great advantage, a special privilege. Besides, they are experienced gamblers !

Where the Protective Tariff doubles freight, and one profit was paid, there is where the money power has centered. Why do the different boards of trade gamble with our products? How long do you think they would gamble with your products, if we had absolute Free Trade? Is there a board of trade in the United States that favors absolute Free Trade? Why not? Simply because it would ruin their splendid business. Do you, an intelligent human being, intend to allow Wall street, the boards of trade, and the Pope of Rome, to still continue to dictate your ballot for you? Do you think it would be possible for capitalists or millionaires to corner your products if we had absolute Free Trade? I say, no! The law of supply and demand would be the only power to regulate the value of your products, and you would only have one direct freight to pay on your products to their destiny.

Wall street and American capitalists have a monopoly on every thing we produce. They have a monopoly on our very existence, and are trying to get a monopoly on our souls! Dear reader, I ask, shall they have a monopoly on your soul, or not?

Political ring leaders keep howling that our Protective Tariff is an injury to England, and other foreign countries that trade with us, and therefore a benefit to the United States. I will gladly admit that our Protective Tariff has been an injury to foreign countries that wanted to trade with us. They have been forced to seek commercial intercourse with less desirable nations on account of our Protective Tariff, and we have lost the best markets in the world for our products. They did not have the mental capacity to think of a better remedy than the vicious McKinley bill and reciprocity, which proved an entire failure. The principal agitators do not even dare to mention the McKinley bill in connection with their glittering promises. Down with the traitors, I say! The traitors to our Constitution; the traitors to "general welfare;" the traitors to "justice" and the prosperity of our nation. If you

are a Republican or a Democrat, don't get excited
and stop reading. I don't blame you for having
been a Republican or a Democrat, but I do blame
you a little for having trusted them as long as
you have. Only a few years ago I was in the
same box, but, thank Fortune, I was not old
enough to vote, and have not yet voted the National ticket, and do not intend to until an absolute Free Trade ticket is in the field.

These same political wolves in sheep's clothes
keep howling that the balance of trade is in our
favor on account of the Protective Tariff. A
blacker and more damnable lie never existed.
The balance of trade can only be governed by
Nature's law of supply and demand. I can tell
you with all candor that, I sincerely believe that
if our ports were thrown wide open to-morrow
and we had absolute Free Trade, that in less
than five years the balance of trade would double
in our favor. There is not a nation on earth, of
any importance, that can produce the variety of
cereals and minerals that we can, and there is
not a prominent nation on earth, of any importance, that could not trade with us advantageously
and yet give us the balance of trade.

Capitalists have taken advantage of our wonderful natural resources, with Protection, to such
an extent that the present disastrous condition of
our country is the result. It is not right it
should be so! We have the greatest country for
natural resources on earth, yet look at our pres-

ent condition! Nearly all trading vessels are
to-day owned by foreign countries. The American traders have been forced to abandon the seas.
As President Cleveland told us all about the cause
in his late message to Congress, it is not necessary for me to go into details on such a minor
question—not only a minor question, dear
reader, but a fictitious one under our present cir-
cumstances. If it had been a question concerning "general welfare," Cleveland would never
have thought about it. It is impossible to provide a permanent remedy under a fictitious system. They can only stimulate with some poison
that will kill in the end! Have we not learned
this in the last thirty years from cause and effect,
that no remedy can be permanent under Protection? I have if you have not. I can tell you
candidly that you need to investigate the condition of our country more closely.

There is not a nation on earth that has absolute Free Trade ; and there is not a nation on
earth that is not at all times forced to change
their laws from one time to another. They raise
their import duties and they lower them, and
sometimes they are obliged to repeal them. They
keep changing their revenue system ; they keep
trying to get permanent remedies, and permanent
systems of taxation to support the government.
But it is utterly impossible for them to do so, so
long as they have a fictitious foundation ; a fictitious system of taxation to support the govern-

ment. Absolute Free Trade is the only foundation on which to build permanent laws and to get a permanent and reliable system of government.

Reader, if you are a farmer, I wish to say to you that you are not benefitted in any way whatever by the Protective Tariff, but on the contrary, as a farmer and original producer you are not only paying more than your share of government expenses, but as farmers you are the people who are adding to the wealth of our millionaires every time you sell a bushel of wheat, corn or any other product of your labor. You are robbing yourself, in favor of capital, every time you sell a pound of your products; every bushel of wheat, corn, or any other cereal you produce you are obliged to sell below its actual value so long as the Protective Tariff exists. It would not be so bad if all the difference went to the support of the government; but not over ten per cent. goes to the government, the other ninety per cent. goes right down into the pockets of protected manufacturers and millionaires. The Protective Tariff causes an extra freight charge on your products, no matter where they are sold. But not over ten per cent. of your products enter foreign markets, and yet you pay that extra freight charge on every pound you produce on account of our import duties. All duties on imports are fictitious, and have been the curse of every nation that ever existed. They simply create wealth for those who have control of protected industries. When

some fictitious stimulant has been applied, nearly
everything seems to go well for a time ; but the
stimulant is poison, and every new disaster becomes worse than the last, and in the end will
bring sure death. It is impossible to use one evil
as a remedy for another ; it can only act as a
temporary stimulant, that cannot effect a permanent cure.

The farmers and original producers are the
original creators of wealth. But whom are you
creating wealth for? For the government? For
yourselves? No! But for those who control protected industries.

The Protective Tariff never was for the purpose of supporting our government or any other
government. It is simply a fictitious form of
taxation for the purpose of giving special privileges to a few, and to shift the burden of taxation
exclusively onto the shoulders of the original producers—farmers and laboring men of the United
States. It is the most expensive form of taxation in existence. It is the most damnable insult to American intelligence in existence. It is
an insult to the fundamental principles of our
Constitution. It is a protector of evil ; a protection for the greatest robbery that has existed
since the dawn of history.

If you are selling wheat to-day for forty cents
per bushel, you are making not over twelve or
thirteen cents per bushel, with the best advan-
tages. The Protective Tariff has caused this un-

reasonable price—which I defy anyone to contradict. With this small profit you have been ex-
pected to support your family; pay taxes to your
local government, pay a Protective Tariff on every
article you consume, create millionaires, support
the merchants and bankers of your town, help
support the churches and charitable institutions
in your neighborhood, and in addition you help
support a foreign institution—the church of
Rome!

And persons benefitted by Protective Tariff
have the impudence to tell you that the Protective Tariff protects the farmers and laboring men
of the United States. Of course it protects you.
They don't lie when they tell you so. They keep
you well protected for their own interests. They
have made you poorer ; they have forced you to
borrow money, place a mortgage on your farm.
One man stands ready with the trap wide open
to protect you in, while others are driving you
into the trap. When they can't drive you into
the trap, they throw out a little bait to coax you
in ! Oh, yes, you are well watched and protected.
My friends, bait is being thrown out while I am
writing these lines. If you must have their bait,
for God's sake don't swallow the hook. I don't
blame you for not voting for Free Trade for the
reason that there has never been an absolute
Free Trade platform in existence. But if it be
the last act of my life, I shall propose an absolute
Free Trade platform that will be in perfect har-

mony with the fundamental principles of the Constitution of the United States, and acceptable to the people.

With absolute Free Trade, you will receive, at the very lowest estimate, one third more for your products. The clothing and other necessaries of life that you buy, will cost you less money than they do to-day,   Only one freight to Liverpool can be charged up against your cereals, hogs, cattle, etc.   And clothing will ·be cheaper because the American manufacturers will not have a monopoly on your trade.   You will have the privilege of buying where you can buy the cheapest, and the privilege of selling where you can get the best price.   Absolute Free Trade means, that you may trade with those who offer you the best trade, or those you want to trade with.   Protection means, that you must pay dearly for the privilege of buying the necessaries of life.   But remember you do not pay the government for these privileges, but you pay every manufacturer that is protected, for the privilege of buying his product, and selling your own.   I defy any one to contradict this statement.

Would it not be unreasonable for the merchants and business men of your town to charge you an admission to enter their places of business to buy the necessaries of life ?   You tell me it certainly would be.   Those, my friend, are the principles ot Protection, only you are forced, besides paying for the privilege of buying from them.

If a person came to you to buy your hogs and told you that they needed your hogs on the market to-day, and that you must sell them to him at his own figures, but first of all you must pay him for the privilege of selling to him, what would you think of such a condition. My friend, those are the fundamental principles of Protection.

It is impossible for me to understand why any merchant or business man in the United States should be in favor of Protection. Is there one merchant in the United States who is benefitted by Protection who is not also a manufacturer and directly benefitted? Who do you depend upon for your patronage and support? Do you depend upon the manufacturers? Do you depend upon the capitalists? Do the manufacturers make any money for you, or do the capitalists make any money for you? If you do not depend upon the manufacturers and capitalists for your support, then you certainly must depend upon the farmers and original producers of wealth. If all the farmers in the United States would quit producing, in less than one year you would not be able to sell one dollar's worth of merchandise, and failure would stare you in the face. And if you still continued to vote for Protection, you would simply receive a just punishment, a just reward!

If you contradict Nature's laws you must always suffer the consequences. Absolute Free Trade—free commercial intercourse—is Nature's greatest and sublimest law of government, but if you substitute Nature's law with a fictitious one, you will suffer in the end. You will bring the disaster upon yourself, and you alone will be to blame.

Protection has made farming repulsive and unprofitable, therefore the young farmers have been driven from the farms to seek more profitable employment. They have entered into the different lines of business ; they have been driven to the cities to seek employment, because the farmers are robbed of their earnings and are not able to pay decent wages. They are forced to work from daylight till dark to make a living. Working on a farm for wages has become the next thing to actual slavery, instead of the most independent and agreeable occupation on earth. You complain of having too much competition, and you have helped to bring the competition upon yourself.

The merchants of the United States are to-day in the same condition as a lot of gamblers who have bled all the suckers and are now obliged to gamble among themselves to make a living. In a short time the less fortunate begin to jump sideways for something to eat. It wont take long for the clever gamblers to spend what they have made, in addition to feeding the less fortunate.

Now, my friend, who will get your wealth in the
end? Those who have special privileges under
Protection. Was Protection for the purpose of
creating a wealthy nation? No—not a wealthy
nation, my friend, not a wealthy government,
but for the purpose of creating a few wealthy
individuals in the nation, and for the purpose of
keeping the common people in poverty, and to
keep our government in financial distress. The
natural resources of the United States are so
great that it has taken a long time to successfully
bring about the present disastrous results. I
personally know that for twenty years the condition of the common people—farmers, merchants
and laboring men—of the United States has become more critical from one year to another.

When a farmer must be in constant fear of
bankruptcy, the merchants are also uncertain.
The farmers and all original producers, the merchants and professional men, and the common
laborers, all have one common interest at heart,
and should all join hands and work in harmony
to down their greatest enemy—the Protective
Tariff.

Selfishness is the greatest evil that can exist.
If it had not been for selfishness we never could
have had Protection, as it contradicts the fundamental teachings of our Constitution Selfishness is fictitious and unnatural and is an enemy
to the highest order of civilization. A selfish
person is not half civilized ! You have a perfect

right to look out for your own interests, but it is your duty to think about the welfare of your posterity and you should try and make the world better for them to live in. Many are the noble men who have sacrificed their lives to better the world for us to live in. But you do not look out for yourselves. You allow capitalists, through Protection, to come right under your nose, and rob the producers of the share of wealth that Nature's laws intended for you.

The same rules hold good with factory hands in the United States as with any other person who depends on his labor for a living. If the farmers and original producers are impoverished it affects the merchants and all professional men as well. If they are not making any money, how can they buy clothing? They will be forced to get along with the cheapest kind, and as small a wardrobe as possible. If they cannot buy the goods manufactured by your employer, where do you expect him to sell his products? Our commercial intercourse with European nations has been ruined, and the producers and consumers of the United States have been impoverished. How can you expect to get steady employment and good wages if it is impossible for your employer to sell his products? My friend, will your employer continue to give you employment if he cannot sell his products? Give the farmers and original producers and laboring men of the United States a chance to become prosperous, and

the products of your labor will have a good market, at home and abroad.

Absolute Free Trade will open and establish our commercial intercourse with the world. European nations have always catered for our trade, because our resources are such that we can supply them with a greater variety than any other nation in the world. There is no other nation that can produce such a large variety of cereals as we can ; and none that can produce so large a variety of material for wearing apparel as we can, and our mineral resources are almost inexhaustible. Leading Protective Tariff agitators have taken advantage of our wonderful resources to gain their own selfish ends : to create a few millionaires, in a few years, to rob our producers of every thing but a living when it was possible. The McKinley bill was the most vicious tariff bill that ever became a law since the dawn of history. It was a million times worse than highway robbery, for the highwayman gives you a chance to see who gets your valuables — and sometimes an opportunity to get them back, or at least a part of them. But the McKinley bill robbed you when you were asleep ; you don't know who got your money, and if you did, it would do you no good, because the robbers are protected and you have no recourse in law.

My friend, I beg of you to take into consideration the future welfare of our nation, yourself and your posterity. Get your friends together, or-

ganize an absolute Free Trade club. Start with
yourself as a member, get good literature, learn
the actual virtues of Free Trade, help organize
when you can, and you and your posterity will
receive a rich reward. Remember that we have
the combined strength of the money power of the
world, and his holiness the Pope of Rome, against
us in this, our fight for absolute Free Trade and
the fundamental principles of the Constitution of
the United States. The pen is mightier than the
sword! It has been used for the purpose of en-
slaving our people, and has so far been successful.
Let us wield the pen for "justice," and we will
come out victorious !

THE SUGAR SCANDAL;

OR THE

FUNDAMENTAL PRINCIPLES OF PROTECTION.

IT IS not necessary for me to enter into details on the sugar scandal in our last Congress. I will simply reproduce two articles that came to my notice in a leading newspaper, dated December 3, 1894, as follows :

"Information from good sources indicate that the German government thinks of levying prohibitory taxes upon American cereals and timber, unless Congress modifies the tariff on German sugar."

And in another column of the same paper I read the following:

"SAN FRANCISCO, CAL., Dec. 2, 1894.—Friday was a red letter day in the history of San Francisco's clearing house. High water mark was reached in a grand total of $1,600,000. There were no great deals on hand, nor did the general run of business indicate that the tidal wave in the commercial history of San Francisco had appeared. The big total was caused by a check signed by Claus Spreckles for $1,500,000, thereby overshadowing the history of financial transactions in the city of many millionaires. Last

evening Claus Spreckles admitted having made
his check for $1,500,000. 'It was drawn on the
Nevada bank,' said he, 'and was made payable to
the Bank of California. It was promptly paid.
There is no special significance in the transaction,
it is only a " little " private matter, in fact, a
family affair. If it had been twenty millions it
would be worth talking about.' "

I don't suppose that any of the readers care
anything about Mr. Spreckles' family affairs, at
least I don't. "If it had been twenty millions it
would be worth talking about," was Mr. Spreckles'
statement when asked about the deal.

But there is something else in connection with
Mr. Spreckles' business that will give us all a
good Free Trade lesson. We now have a prohibitory duty on German sugar for the purpose
of creating millionaires at the expense of the people. Our government does not get one cent of
duty from German sugar, for our duty is prohibitory. The German product is acknowledged to
be far superior to the sugar we now consume.
The prohibitory duty against the German product gives Mr. Spreckles and other American refiners an opportunity to raise the price of their
product from its real value to the same level as
the prohibitory duty on German sugar, and they
now get more for their inferior product than the
German sugar would cost you, which is far superior. Therefore you are paying a fancy price for
an inferior article. You are paying a duty on
every pound of sugar you consume, not to our

government, but to Mr. Spreckles and other sugar refiners. You are paying them a fancy price for the privilege of buying their inferior sugar. In other words you are forced to buy from them and forced to pay for the privilege of buying from them.

The principal object to-day with the sugar refiners, and all protected industries, is to be protected for the purpose of making larger profits on their products. The result is that they are not obliged to keep their mills running more than half the time to make a handsome profit on their investments. Their products cost you more money, therefore you are forced to economize ; you are not able to consume such a large quantity as you would like to because of high prices. The consequence is that it creates a surplus of labor. They produce faster than we are able to consume, because of high prices. Therefore a surplus of labor is created. They produce faster than we can consume, because of high prices, and when there is a surplus of labor, labor is always cheap. Supply and demand regulates the price of labor just the same as with any commodity. The whole Protective Tariff scheme has been to create cheap labor for the industries that are protected !

It has only taken Mr. Spreckles a few years to make his millions, under Protection, at our expense. Can we blame the German government if they levy prohibitory duty on our cereals and timber? What will the result be if they do? My friend, our cereals and timber must fall in value, for the demand will become dull. Our cereals and timber cannot be sold in Germany and the result will be lower prices for our products. I would not blame the German government if they did not buy another dollar's worth of our products. They certainly will not buy any more than they are absolutely obliged to.

The foregoing was not the sugar scandal, it was simply a sample of everyday occurrences.

I will now give you a sample taste of American sugar of to-day. It is not necessary for me to elaborate on the sugar scandal in Congress to give you the largest dose of sweetness that you ever took. Even President Cleveland was obliged to condemn it ; even his hardened conscience could not face the shame without making an excuse. Our present Congress, following in the footsteps of our former Congress, is simply the tool for capitalists to gain their ends. Congress was willing to give us free raw materials, to mislead us, and then place a prohibitory duty on refined sugar—simply shifting us from the frying pan into the fire. But, thank Fortune, we are not so ignorant as they believed us to be. What does free raw material mean, so long as we prohibit refined sugar? It simply means a stronger clutch by capital on the American producers and consumers. It means that American refiners of sugar will have no competition at all.

Mr. Spreckles can bring his raw sugar from the
Hawaiian Islands to San Francisco free of duty.
His refineries are located in San Francisco, where
the sugar is refined and enters the American
market free of duty, and he can sell at any price
decided on by the Sugar Trust, within the limit
of the prohibitory duty on German sugar. Have
the American people ever taken a larger dose of
sweetness? Is there an American citizen so blind
that he cannot see what the Protective Tariff is
for? There is only one way to prohibit capital
from robbing the people, and that is to have
absolute Free Trade, with a better source of
revenue for the support of the government. If
you trace the sugar scandal to its origin you will
find that without Protection it would be impossible for such a condition to exist. Every great
scheme for robbing the people, indirectly, is
backed up by Protection, and no man in the
United States dares attempt to prove the contrary.
I defy any man in the United States to prove the
contrary, and give me the same opportunity to
answer that they will have to attack. They are
cowards! They would not dare to let me answer
through the columns of a red-hot Republican
paper. I defy them!

The Protective Tariff is at the root of *every*
evil that exists in our government affairs to-day.
If I had the time and means to write a large book,
I would take one evil at a time and trace the
origin to Protection. Not in the United States

alone, but the world over, and our government has the most vicious system of them all. The Pope of Rome understood his business and selected the United States as the best field for operation. With absolute Free Trade and strict adherence to the fundamental principles of our Constitution, the Pope would be as helpless as a child, within the borders of the United States.

THE HOWL OF OVER-PRODUCTION

AND

FOREIGN IMMIGRATION.

W E often hear the misleading cry of over-production in the United States. My friend, I
say with all candor, and base my statement on facts
that can not be disputed, that there would never
be an over-production in the United States if the
original creators of wealth were not robbed of all
the wealth they create. Whenever the laboring
men or consumers, in the United States, are doing well and making money, we never hear the
cry of over-production; there is always a brisk
and ready market for the products of our country.
But there is even a more important side of the
question to be taken into consideration : There
could never be any over-production if the farmer
received a reasonable price for his products. The
farmer is not in love with hard work and long
hours any more than the merchant or any other
person, not excepting the common laborer. Protection has caused low prices, and low prices
have forced him to cultivate and produce more
to make enough money to pay his taxes and get

a half-way respectable living. I was raised on an Illinois farm and have lived in different parts of some of the best farming sections in the United States, and have had a little experience in farming myself, therefore know what I am talking about. I know that you cannot pick one farmer out of every one hundred that will work hard unless he is actually forced to do so through necessity. There are very few farmers that have not been forced to increase their acreage for cultivation through actual and forced necessity. Who has forced them to do so? I say the Protectionists, through the capitalists. Can you contradict me? If you can, and will, I will appreciate it. Why have they forced them? For the purpose of making a brisk market for their money at a high rate of interest. In other words, to get a mortgage on their homes, to keep them in submission, and in the end to own their homes and be the landlords. The capitalists don't want money, they want your homes, they want wealth. Money is simply their agent to accomplish their evil purposes. Money in itself is not wealth. I have heard very smart men say: "Give me the money and you may have the land and property." But, my friend, a person who makes such a statement don't know enough to stay inside when it rains. Such persons do not realize that all the money in the United States would not be a drop in the bucket towards paying for the wealth represented by our millionaires alone!

Reader, I am willing at any time to stake my life that with absolute Free Trade the capitalists will be entirely powerless to rob you, without your finding it out in short order, and then you will have recourse in law.

The great, great howl among Protectionists in the United States to-day is, that foreign immigration is the cause of the present critical condition among the people. It is simply a fictitious howl, intended to mislead the people from the real cause ; and I hope that there is no man in the United States so ignorant as to believe such a foolish and idiotic statement.

If there were fifty men in my county and fifty men in your county, and twenty-five in each county were manufacturing, and the other twenty-five farmers or producers, and ten of my manufacturers emigrate to your county and enter into the business of manufacturing, I would have ten less of manufacturers ; therefore a deficiency of ten manufacturers, which gives me ten more producers than I need. But you have got my ten manufacturers added to yours, which gives you a shortage of ten producers to supply the manufacturers, and then trade must begin. You have a surplus of manufactured articles and a deficiency of cereals ; I have a surplus of cereals and a deficiency of manufactured articles ; therefore we simply exchange products and the result will be the same as before emigration started.

If fifty thousand foreigners come to the United

States, and they should all happen to be farmers,
there would be fifty thousand farmers or producers less in Europe. They would simply become producers in the United States to supply
the deficiency of products in Europe. If fifty
thousand factory hands should come from Europe
to the United States, there would simply be fifty
thousand more in the United States to supply the
deficiency of factory hands in Europe.

Immigration should not be prohibited! It
should be encouraged instead. It is true that
there are certain classes of immigrants that
should be prohibited from landing in the United
States, and especially persons who cannot read
and write their own language, including crim-
inals and ex-convicts. If we pass laws to prohibit
immigration, to impoverish the people in foreign
countries, we would simply be jumping from the
frying pan into the fire. It would be a fictitious
law, contrary to Nature, and there would be evil
results. You may ask why it is not fictitious to
prohibit undesirable immigrants as well? For the
simple reason that Nature's best teachings demand of us to purify our government. Nature's
best teachings are opposed to ignorance, immor-
ality and vice.

If we pass fictitious laws to prohibit immigration, we impoverish the people of those countries;
and the impoverishment of those people mean
no market for our products. When we bar out
the foreigners, and bar out foreign trade with

Protection, we simply force them to seek more profitable trade with other nations, and force them to encourage other nations to increase their productions. We are simply bringing disaster upon ourselves.

ORIGIN OF OUR HIGH PROTECTIVE TARIFF;

THE

CAUSE AND EFFECT.

IT IS not my object to write a history of Protection and its origin, as it would take up more time than I have to spare at present, and more space than I can afford to pay for. My object is not to stuff the reader with dates and statistics, but with plain, unadulterated facts that can not be disputed.

The Protective Tariff always originates with a nation in its first stage of corruption. At first the Tariff is limited to only a few articles, and the people do not realize the danger of Protection, but go to sleep and slumber sweetly until the day of "judgment" comes, until the terrible disaster is upon them ; and the awakening, with

many powerful nations, has been too late,   Shall
it be too late with us, or shall it not?   We await
your answer.

The Protective Tariff is always supposed to be
for the purpose of supporting the government,
but the origin of our High Protective Tariff was
for the purpose of fostering infant industries, or
giving special privileges to a few at the expense
of the people.   Of course we were not told that it
would be at the expense of the people, or that
anyone was to have special privileges.   They
simply forgot to tell us that part of the story and
we are therefore not supposed to know.

You may ask why I say that the origin of our
High Protective Tariff was not for the purpose of
supporting our government.   My answer is, that
it was not necessary.   Better forms of taxation
for the support of our government have at different times been proposed to our legislators, and
particularly at the close of our late war, but none
were acceptable, to a majority of our legislators,
that would not protect and give special privileges
to their pets—infant industries.

These same infant industries have been protected until they have become gigantic concerns,
until they now have billions of dollars to back
them up.   With the aid of Wall street and high
priced whiskey they now have almost complete
control of the press in the United States.   There
is not a Democratic Free Trade newspaper in the
United States to-day that advocated Free Trade

during our last Presidential campaign. New York capital to-day controls the financial condition of the people in the United States. You, reader, are one of their slaves!

I want every reader to understand that I do not blame the capitalists for taking advantage of existing laws that give them special privileges, but I do blame them for bribing our representatives for the purpose of getting still greater privileges.

The Protective Tariff in the United States will be written in history as the most vicious form of taxation that ever existed!

It is not very strange that the principal Protective Tariff agitators entered into the industries that in reality were protected. Have any of them become farmers? No; and why not? If they had wanted to become farmers I am willing to stake my life that to-day we would have absolute Free Trade, with a simple and inexpensive form of taxation for the support of our government. Politicians took advantage of American patriotism at the close of our late war to get complete control of the products of labor to speculate with. They told the people that the Protective Tariff would give them all an opportunity to become wealthy! Have any of you laborers and farmers become millionaires? Why not? There was an opportunity; others became millionaires, and why not you? These same men now represent the money power of the United States. They,

have laughed at the people for being so ignorant
as to let them pull the wool over their eyes ; but
he that laughs last laughs best !

It grieves me to think that an intelligent people like the citizens of the United States, with the
privilege of untrammeled thought, free speech
and a right to give their judgment power, can be
so careless about the general welfare of humanity
and their posterity, as to listen to a dictatorship,
and not take the question in their own hands to
investigate and pass their own judgment upon.
I would like to see the day when every town and
village would have organizations for the purpose
of discussing or debating on questions of government—not a party organization, but an organization where all can meet together and discuss the
leading questions, to better the condition of humanity.   Partisan strife is one of our greatest
enemies.   When a person becomes so patriotic
to one party that he will not stop to reason or
listen to the principles of opposing political
parties, it is really too bad.   I pity such persons;
they can only expect in the end to be betrayed
for their loyalty.   A wise man may change his
mind, but a fool never !

I want to impress upon the minds of the
readers that I do not call a man a fool who does
not believe the way I do.   Every person, after
making a thorough investigation, has a perfect
right to form his own opinion ; but he has no

right to form an opinion until he has made an investigation.

If your party is in the wrong, or has been, do you, an intelligent human being, expect them to come to you and tell you so? It is natural for an individual to try and hide his faults, and just as natural for him to show his best qualities. If the rule holds good with one person, why not with a political party, or even a nation? I claim that they are a thousand times more apt to hide their faults, if possible. It very often happens that one child in a family will lose all self-respect, and all respect for his people. He may become a worthless wretch, but the family pride will try to hide his faults and keep up his reputation until it becomes utterly hopeless.

The American people are broad-minded and liberal in their views on every other subject that comes before them ; why not in politics ? Why not take up and investigate every reform proposed ? A person who will not admit that there is always room for improvement is either a fool or an idiot. If any of the proposed reforms are good, we want them ; if they are bad, throw them aside, and we will be wiser for having investigated.

THE DEMOCRATIC PARTY NOT A. FREE TRADE PARTY.

AS AN absolute Free Trader I denounce the Democratic party as a faking party and fraud of the worst kind, and not worthy of the support of true and honest Democrats. Their National platform does not declare for Free Trade, as a great. many people believe who have not taken the. trouble to read the platform, but simply favors Tariff Reform and Reciprocity. But through the press and political orators the people were lead to believe that Democratic success meant Free Trade, and the Free Trade vote elected our last President. Did we get Free Trade? Republican orators told us that Democratic success meant Free Trade and the ruination of the United States.

I wish to ask how it is possible to have Protection and Free Trade at the same time? If the people had not been deceived by false promises of Free Trade by the Democratic press and orators, and misleading insinuations by the Republican press and orators, the two old parties would have finished their grave digging ready for burial.

For the fiscal year ending June 30, 1894, there was a deficit, in the United States Treasury, of $69,803,260.58. The government has so far issued $100,000,000 in bonds to help pay the necessary expenses, and without a doubt will be obliged to make another large bond issue before President Cleveland's term expires. This, my friend, is the result of Democratic and Republican faking combined. They have learned that the tendency among the people is for absolute Free Trade. The Democratic party has not been a Free Trade party in reality for years, except in name. Both of the old parties have combined to do all in their power to down the tendency for Free Trade, and the Democratic party has simply been the tool to blind the people who wanted Free Trade. I do not blame a Republican for not voting the Democratic ticket, for it is simply a fake, and I do not blame Democrats for not wanting to vote the Republican ticket, for the principles of the Republican party have always been fictitious, but I do blame Free Traders for continuing to place any confidence in the Democratic party, which left the true principles of Democracy long before it came to life, or an existence. Democracy was bred of virtue but born a bastard. Republicanism was born of virtue but has lived the life of, and will die, a bastard.

The McKinley Bill was the most vicious system of taxation that ever became a law, but I would have been well pleased to see it in effect during one more administration, for then, it would not matter how blind the people are, they would have been thoroughly convinced of the vicious, fictitious fraud of Protection. Millions of people in the United States, who still have a small claim left to their homes, would have been ruined, starved and robbed of the interests that they still hold. Could there be a better argument against Protection? Some people must be starved before they would give up an old idea that their father told them was the best in the world. They are so ignorant that they think their fathers knew everything that was worth knowing. Necessity is the mother of invention. They must simply be forced by starvation before they care to learn anything their fathers and dictators have not told them. I don't like to see people starve, but it would be a good thing for humanity if every man did starve enough to find out that there are things worth knowing that their fathers did not know, and that their fathers are just as apt to be mistaken as any other person.

The $100,000,000 bond issue by our Democratic administration was caused by reductions on tariffs, and has saved some of the people from starving quite enough to open their eyes. If the McKinley bill had continued in effect for one more administration the Protective Tariff doctrine would have been dead and buried deep into oblivion, never to rise again as a political issue, but would simply have a place in history as a *warning against Protection* to our posterity, and to all humanity.

The principal supporters of Protection knew of the terrible disaster they were bringing on themselves, and were only too glad to shift the responsibility on to the Democratic party. They wanted to get rid of the McKinley bill but did not dare to repeal the law themselves, for they would simply be digging their own graves. They did not want Free Trade, and were only too glad to get the ghost of a show to shift the responsibility on to any party that was not a Free Trade party, that could possibly be successful.

Dear reader, so long as you continue to vote the Republican or Democratic ticket I hope that you will get the full benefit of these hard times ; that you will get your full share of disaster that you are helping to bring down on humanity. My sympathy goes out for you ; I pity you. But as ye sow, so shall ye reap. I only hope that those who are not guilty would not be forced to take the same reward, but could be rewarded according to their labors.

What does Free Trade mean ? I claim that if it means anything it means absolute Free Trade. A fictitious issue, called Free Trade, has been agitated before the people for years, so that the majority of people would lose the true meaning of the words, Free Trade. I can say candidly that the two old parties are combined to keep the

people in ignorance of the true meaning of Free
Trade. They do not give us absolute Free Trade
for even one administration, for they could never
have Protection again. Protection would forever
be a dead issue in the United States! Absolute
Free Trade means the fundamental principles of
our Constitution, and the fundamental principles
of our Constitution are Justice, Domestic Tranquility, Prosperity and *General Welfare*. They dare
not give us " general welfare " for a term of four
years, for the people would then find out what it
means, and would be too well satisfied to ever
want Protection again. Protection is fictitious ;
based on selfishness and supported by ignorance.
Free Trade is natural ; based on justice and supported by intelligence.

Abraham Lincoln said : You can fool some of
the people all the time ; most of the people some
of the time, but you cannot fool all of the people ·
all the time. Why did Abraham Lincoln make
this statement ? When did he make this statement, and to whom did he make this statement ?
Was he talking to the people, or was he talking
to our representatives ? Would it be reasonable
to think that he made such a statement to the
people ? My friend, if you will take the pains to
look up past records you will find that the statement was made by Lincoln to our representatives
concerning the Protective Tariff. Abraham Lincoln has been placed before us as a model and
noble man, which he certainly was, and then his
statements were misconstrued to deceive the
people.

THE PEOPLE'S PARTY PLATFORM.

The People's Party platform favors and demands some very good reforms, but the people have been misled. The fundamental principles of their platform are fictitious, and leave an opportunity for opposing parties to find fault and attack their principles ; and they should be attacked so long as they do not harmonize with the fundamental principles of our Constitution.

The demand for the graduated income tax is fictitious ; it is unjust; it is class legislation. If we tax capital for the special privileges they have had in the past, we must expect to continue to give them special privileges. It is ridiculous ! If we tax special privileges we must foster them. You must give them some special privilege for the extra burden of taxation imposed upon them.

Our Republican and Democratic representatives are willing to aid with any fictitious law the People's Party wishes to propose. Has it not been proven to you?

The reform party must be just in every way. They must not be selfish, nor teach the people to be selfish. The people must not think for one minute that they must take the advantage of capital to get even, for then they will simply be bringing a worse disaster upon themselves. Justice must be dealt out to capitalists and all alike. To be revengeful is dangerous. What do you care how much money or wealth the capitalists have, so long as you get justice and an opportunity to become prosperous? The people must simply demand justice to all, and special privileges to none, and no more. Why not start aright? Why not start at the bottom and remove the principal cause of every evil that exists in the United States to-day—Protection? You certainly do not expect to get wealth without earning or creating wealth. Let the capitalists have their wealth. Let them accumulate wealth so long as they have no chance to rob you of your just earnings. Free Trade will not stop the capitalists from accumulating wealth, but it will stop them from robbing you of the wealth you have produced and accumulated. It will give you an opportunity to sell your products where you can get the best price without paying more than one freight. You will not be obliged to pay more than the actual value for the necessaries of life that you consume.

Free Trade will open and establish our commercial intercouse with the leading nations of the world. It is not impossible for the farmers and stock raisers of our country to sell their products to-day, but it is impossible for them to sell and make a profit. Protection has ruined our commercial intercourse with the leading nations of the world, and we have been forced to try reciprocity to find a market for our products. There is no over-production.

THE FINANCIAL QUESTION.

A GREAT many persons are lead to believe that the only remedy for the present critical condition of the United States is the free and un-limited coinage of silver. My friend, if you believe such teachings you do not understand the true condition of government affairs to-day. Who would Free Silver benefit ? First of all the capi-talists, who own the silver mines, and next the men who work the mines, which is all very well as far as it goes. The miners need work; but without absolute Free Trade first of all there can never be a reliable and safe Financial system in the United States. The free and unlimited coin-age of silver would, without a doubt, help the mining districts and the country surrounding them ; but it would be like the poisonous drug which is used as a stimulant. It would simply

be a fictitious stimulant that would kill in the
end.

So long as our present fictitious system of
government exists, a perfectly reliable and just
financial system can never be established until
the true principles of our Constitution are carried
out to the letter.

It don't matter how much money there is in
the country if the people have not created wealth
as security for money, for, as I have said before,
money in itself is not wealth but merely a temporary representative. If the amount of circu-
lating medium was increased to one hundred
dollars per capita within one year, it would only
act as a temporary stimulant, for under the present fictitious system the financial conspirators
can control a large circulation just as easily as
they can the present amount of money, which is
only $24.05 per capita. In the year 1885 the
per capita amounted to over $35. We need more
money to properly handle the business of the
country. But let us begin at the root of all evil
and make a clean sweep by abolishing all indirect
taxation to get a reliable and substantial foundation to build upon. The United States government should have the full control of the financial
affairs of this country, but it can never, get that
control so long as indirect taxation exists. Ever
since the birth of our republic, financial legislation has been agitating the people and they have
never yet been able to create a safe system. The

wheels of industry in the United States could be stopped in forty-eight hours if the financial conspirators should choose to stop them.

Reader, I ask, have we ever had a safe and reliable form of government under Protection? Have we ever had a safe financial system? I say no, and defy any man in the United States to successfully contradict me.

My friend, it is hard to give up and deny the virtues of the cradle we have been rocked in, even when we find out that it never had any virtues. It is hard to give up the teachings of our childhood, even when we learn that they are fictitious and wrong. But it will be better in the end if we do. A wise man will change his mind, but a fool, never. There are a great many prominent men in the United States who have changed their minds and have not made it public. To such I will say, the sooner you make it known to the public the better it will be for yourself, your posterity and the rest of humanity. A word from you will have an influence with your associates.

If this Message has revealed anything new to you in favor of absolute Free Trade, please don't be selfish, but let some friend read the contents of this pamphlet—pass it around. I am not writing

to make a fortune, but to try to help better the
condition of the people in the United States.
The greater number of persons each pamphlet
reaches, the greater will be my reward. I will
appreciate the result of my labor that much more.

The Republican party is like a cannon well
loaded with powder, but no ball. The cannon
was fired by Protective Tariff agitators. The terrible report was Protection, directed at "supposed
enemies." The echo was the McKinley bill, and
the people have just found out that the cannon
was not loaded, that Protection was merely a sham
battle, and that they have been supporting a
sham battle that has just been wasting powder on
"supposed enemies" who, in "reality," are our
"real friends."

The Democratic party is like the man who
started in business on a very large scale. The
man was dishonest and unjust half of the time
and honest and just the other half of his time.
He did not divide his time into hours or days,
but was honest one minute and dishonest the
next. The consequence was that all his custom-
ers lost their confidence in him for they did not
know when to trust him. The man has now
failed in business. The sheriff (Cleveland) has
the keys and is selling his merchandise out to
the highest bidder.

The People's Party is like an orphan that has adopted parents, where very poor judgment has been used in selecting them ; for the nature of the child is entirely different from that of its adopted parents — the adopted parents have reached their majority, and have established characters and dispositions. As the nature and disposition of the child is entirely different, it will receive a fictitious education at the hands of its adopted parents, which is contrary to the nature and disposition of the child. Possibly, too late in life the child will learn, to its sorrow, that it has received a fictitious education.

Reader, decide :—

A GOVERNMENT OF THE PEOPLE, BY THE PEOPLE, FOR THE PEOPLE.

OR

A GOVERNMENT OF THE MILLIONAIRES, BY THE MILLIONAIRES, FOR THE MILLIONAIRES.

Yours for Justice, Prosperity, Domestic Tranquility and General Welfare,

"A SUCKER."

www.ingramcontent.com/pod-product-compliance
Lightning Source LLC
Chambersburg PA
CBHW020253290326
41930CB00039B/1205